# NO LONGER AN INGENUE

By Megan D Robinson

BLUE LIGHT PRESS ◆ 1ST WORLD PUBLISHING

1st WORLD
PUBLISHING

SAN FRANCISCO ◆ FAIRFIELD ◆ DELHI

**Winner of the 2014 Blue Light Poetry Prize**

# NO LONGER AN INGENUE

Copyright ©2014 by Megan D Robinson

1ST WORLD LIBRARY
PO Box 2211
Fairfield, Iowa 52556
www.1stworldpublishing.com

BLUE LIGHT PRESS
www.bluelightpress.com
Email: bluelightpress@aol.com

BOOK & COVER DESIGN
Melanie Gendron

COVER ART
"Self Portrait" by Megan D Robinson

COVER PHOTOGRAPH
Corwin Robinson

AUTHOR PHOTOGRAPH
Taken at Summer Fishtrap, 2012, Enterprise, OR

FIRST EDITION

ISBN: 978-1-59540-954-6

# TABLE OF CONTENTS

# Real Men Date Doormats

Don't know where I lost it
but there it was
dusty and forgotten
lying in a cobwebby corner
at the backside of my brain
pummeled to death with good intentions,
fearful humility and greed for acceptance,
which I thought could only come
by stopping up my voice with
sticky threads of self-denial.

I found my voice today
and it is loud:
powerful and gentle,
joyous and painful,
raucous and refined.
I'm full of contradictions,
finding what I already had,
singing in a voice I'd never lost
but just forgotten.
Or felt somehow,
in the interests of self-preservation,
I should put a lid on it.
Well a voice is to be used
so I will yell
till it echoes in the hills.
No more mousing around for this girl.
Ha.

I found my voice today.
Don't know where I lost it.
Have my suspicions
I set it aside
out of fear of losing love,
as if real men only date doormats.

Found my voice today
You're gonna hear it.
I ain't gonna shut up,
not for love or money.
Found my voice today
and I'm never gonna lose it again.

## Song

You sing to me
as my heart sings within me
of the hills of my body.
I look
and indeed, there are hills and valleys,
mountains and meadows,
places where light and dark
dance in shadow.

My heart blooms.
I stand hip deep
amid roses and lilies,
gardenias and violets twined
in my hair, and I sing of the hills of my body
to you.

# Why Do You Tremble?

Are you afraid
I mean it literally when I say I could eat you for dessert?
Be assured, I am a vegetarian.
Are you afraid
like Ishtar
I will love you to death?
I promise I would journey
down to Hell to fetch you.
Do I smell of blood and secrets?
Do I smell of wind and tree song?
Are you afraid of the lightning
in my hips as I undulate across the room?
Was it my howling at the moon
in a pink party dress
without the decency
to run naked through Chautauqua Park?
Perhaps the cauldron on the hearth
and my saddled broom stick?
Is it the poetry?
My speaking in wild tongues,
the serpents wound around my wrists?
I assure you, they will not bite—
well, maybe just a nip.
Is it the dirt between my toes,
the fact I do not shave,
my conversations with trees?

Perhaps you are afraid,
in a fit of pique,
that I might run you through.
My sword is only bamboo
and I'd have to push really hard.
I hold a pomegranate in my hands.
Be courageous.
Take a bite.

## Release

My memory shattered like glass
which reached the breaking point
as the fender hit my ribs
and everything remains still to me
like a dream shared by others
which requires a password
in a language unknown to me
to truly understand.
All I know is that something
was released
in that bone shattering night
as my femur cracked in spirals
and my head sprung leaks
as I communed with concrete
angels and asphalt demi-gods
who told me secrets unknown and unknowable.
I came back from their dark embrace
safeguarded through the night in the
womb of an avian automobile
airlifted to sanity in Iowa City
where doctors believe in the sacred grounding of touch.

My smile had shaken free of some dark past
and I've spent months guiltily trying
to hide its brilliance, afraid to glory in my transformation
labeled horrible by those who don't know what wisdom
lies inherent in fenders and is communicated through
blood loss and gravel rock speech, the tongues of earth.
I slide gradually back into the rhythm of my body
and am amazed at whose open hands
have my heart.

# Vertigo

Will you run
when you know
my stomach dances the quadrille
at the sound of your voice?
Would you laugh to know
I am afraid I was made
to fit you?
My cheek shaped
to press against your sternum,
my breasts made for your cupped hands,
my arms built with your circumference in mind?
Will your family convince you
I am too far away to love you?
Are you afraid I will turn to stone?
I think your back is strong enough to rest my heart on.
I am a riddle with many questions.
Can you hear me singing your name over 1400 miles,
or will I surprise your dreams?
I come to you,
the fey girl relinquishing the wild
for a home.

## Metamorphosis

Silken strands of hair fall to my feet.
The sound of broken glass echoes in my ears.
Bald as a newborn,
my past swept into newspapers
and thrown out with the trash,
I wait in bridal splendor for my initiation.

# Surprises Happen

You didn't know
I felt abortion personally abhorrent,
I wanted so badly
to follow your path
of righteousness,
I said "yes"
while my gut screamed
"No, run away,
have this baby in the wilderness,
he is your sacred trust."
Self-preservation possessed me
on the morning of my death,
threw me on a train to safety.
I left my life
still knit into yours,
our books, our crockery and clothing
still sharing space.

Conception
is an occupational hazard
of sex. You chose the possibility
of life every time you loved me
when I was wet and fertile once a month.
Planned families are a wonderful idea.
Surprises happen.

## Supernova

> " What is to give light must endure burning"
> —Victor Frankel

Your words' barbed edges still quiver
beneath the flesh of my heart,
your hatred a cooling weight
I feel obliged to carry.

I forget I ran for liberation.
I escaped to save our son,
the life you wished to terminate
at gestation. I crossed you —
never cross paths with a moving train.
I was a bad girl.
I stayed pregnant.

Now I am a woman
with a four-year-old you want to father.
Suddenly he is your soul.
I am supposed to forget
those blistering phone calls,
though my ears still burn
from your invectives.
I am supposed to forget
you told the DHS I was an unfit parent
while you smoked dope after teaching kindergarten.

I have spent too much time apologizing,
defending you, excusing you,
believing I deserved your hatred
since I dared to conceive without your consent.

This bitterness is a weight
I must set aside.

If I relinquish my camouflage
and dance in the fire,
your words cannot hurt me.
I will absorb them into my own flame
as I go nova,
releasing the restraint caused
living in time
to other peoples' lies and expectations.

There will always be predators.
I am not prey.
No longer satisfied to live
a moving target,
I step into my glory.
I have remembered the purpose of being burned —
to be reborn.

# Love Chemo

I need my marrow removed
to pull you from the inside of my bones,
my cells recalibrated,
reset to eradicate my body's yearning,
a brain rinse
to wash you from my thoughts,
to cleanse away the rat-trap
reliving of old arguments.

I need a spiritual exfoliation,
a specially re-formulated mud-mask
to suck you from my pores.
I need to excise the lingering disease
of our so-called love
and attain remission.

## A Mother-Baby Yin-Yang

We sit amid a scaffolding of pillows,
his weight shored up
by eiderdown and poly-fill,
his supine form curled
around my belly like a comma,
my arms
pillowing his head and knees.
Caught in the aftermath of nursing,
smiles of dreamy satiation flicker
at the edges of his mouth
in time to my heart.

## Writer's Block

Poems burn my fingertips,
pushing to get out.
Full of frustrated creativity,
I lose patience with my child.
I can't finish breakfast —
he's desperate for moo.
I can't write while nursing —
it distracts him.
I can't write while we play
on the quilt in the living room —
he'd rather chew on my bright
shiny pen or gum the edges of my journal.
When I try to write
curled in the rocking chair
while he gleefully disassembles
a newspaper,
great crocodile tears
stream down his cheeks —
I am too far away.

# Cindergirl

My mother doesn't understand
my need for camouflage —
the tattered sweats,
the unkempt hair,
all make me safely nondescript.
Potentially repellent, even.
She wants me dancing
in a star-spangled dress
the color of midnight,
safe in the arms of a man,
any man.

But I have learned
the danger of attraction;
there are still verbal boot prints
fading from my spine.
I know well that beauty can be dangerous
in what it attracts.
Better to hide,
a menial shadow
in ill-fitting clothes.

I know the cost
of unequal love,
raising my son ¾ alone,
only the threat of a restraining order

stopping his father's vitriolic phone calls.
Operating in survival mode,
I have no time for frivolity.
Any resurgent desire
to be belle of the ball
is firmly squelched.

My soul dies of root rot,
stifled by the endless monotony,
with no music
or fripperies,
or flirtations,

no watercolors,
or sculpting clay.
I shift in the cage
I've built for protection
ready to pull out of this disguise
and bloom.

# Self-excavation

*Live your passions*, shouts
the earnest young man,
hounding me through Natural Selections
as I leave the cash register,
pass shelves of neatly folded
organic cotton underwear,
and clock out.

He insists this will solve all my problems.
The insomnia, the food sensitivities,
the chronic weight-loss,
the unexplained jaundice,
the depression.

I remember being filled
with such righteous zeal.
Fresh out of college
I was going to change the world
through installation art, poetry,
and a commitment
to local, organic produce.

That was before the Volvo
slammed into me that icy night.
Life gave me unexpected permutations;
I am a disabled single parent
with a brain injury, chronic fatigue,
and a pre-adolescent son

who eats more than I do.

To live my passions
I have to find them
in a low-lying fog.
Moving requires extreme
conscious effort;
muscles rubbery with fatigue,
as if shot up with Novocain.

The words
I once loved slide
like greased marbles
in my mouth, refusing
to match any logical sequence.

Motherhood has become
an incessant round of taxi service
to soccer games, play dates,
and field trips.

I have a wonderful son,
but not the husband I expected,
though many of my married friends
could say the same.

I struggle to excavate myself,
pushing through the numbness
with each small gratitude.

## Ball Gown Optional

I hunger
for brightly colored
eye shadow, body glitter,
and evening wear more exciting
than flannel pajamas.

It´s time to shake
the cobwebs from my hair,
wipe the dust bunnies
from my sleeves,
straighten my spine
and walk
like a dancer again.

I am ready
to shine like the stars,
ball gown optional,
even
while I dance
tatter-coated among the geese.

# About the Author

Megan is a poet, performance artist, freelance writer, locavore, gluten-free kitchen witch, and single parent. She lives with her teen-aged son and their supernaturally cute Pomeranian. Her work has been published in the *Iowa Source*, *The Ottumwa Courier*, the anthology *Lyrical Iowa 2007*, and the anthology *This Enduring Gift*. She is passionate about poetry as performance art and looks forward to sharing her work at an open mike near you.

## Acknowledgments

"Metamorphosis" and "Song" were previously published in *This Enduring Gift*, 2010 (1st World Publishing)

"A Mother-Baby Yin Yang" was previously published in *Lyrical Iowa 2007*, (The Iowa Poetry Association)